W9-AOA-082

DINOSAURS

APATOSAURUS

A 4D Book

by Tammy Gagne

PEBBLE
a capstone imprint

Easy
567.91 GAG

Download the Capstone 4D app!

- Ask an adult to download the Capstone 4D app.

- Scan the cover and stars inside the book for additional content.

When you scan a spread, you'll find fun extra stuff to go with this book! You can also find these things on the web at www.capstone4D.com using the password: apat.95520

Pebble Plus is published by Pebble,
1710 Roe Crest Drive, North Mankato, Minnesota 56003
www.mycapstone.com

Library of Congress Cataloging-in-Publication Data
Names: Gagne, Tammy, author.
Title: Apatosaurus : a 4D book / by Tammy Gagne.
Description: North Mankato, Minnesota : an imprint of Pebble, [2019] |
Series: Pebble plus. Dinosaurs | Audience: Age 4–8.
Identifiers: LCCN 2018002951 (print) | LCCN 2018009262 (ebook) |
ISBN 9781515795643 (eBook PDF) | ISBN 9781515795520 (hardcover) |
ISBN 9781515795582 (paperback)
Subjects: LCSH: Apatosaurus—Juvenile literature.
Classification: LCC QE862.S3 (ebook) | LCC QE862.S3 G3373 2019 (print)
| DDC 567.913/8—dc23
LC record available at https://lccn.loc.gov/2018002951

Editorial Credits
Hank Musolf, editor; Charmaine Whitman, designer;
Kelly Garvin, media researcher; Laura Manthe, production specialist;
Illustrator, Capstone Press/Jon Hughes

Design Elements
Shutterstock/Krasovski Dmitri

Printed and bound in China.
000309

Note to Parents and Teachers

The Dinosaurs set supports the national science standards related to life science. This book describes and illustrates apatosaurus. The images support early readers in understanding the text. The repetition of words and phrases helps early readers learn new words. This book also introduces early readers to subject-specific vocabulary words, which are defined in the Glossary section. Early readers may need assistance to read some words and to use the Table of Contents, Glossary, Read More, Internet Sites, Critical Thinking Questions, and Index sections of the book.

Table of Contents

Meet the Apatosaurus

Apatosaurus was one of the biggest dinosaurs. It was about 70 feet (21 meters) long. It weighed more than 20 tons (18 metric tons). That is more than two elephants!

The dinosaur's four legs were as big as tree trunks. Its back feet had more claws than its front feet.

Apatosaurus had a long neck and tail. Its head was small. The apatosaurus' sharp teeth broke plants apart.

A Big Meal for a Big Dinosaur

The apatosaurus needed to eat lots

of food. It ate about 800 pounds

(360 kilograms) of plants

each day. It was an herbivore.

Apatosaurus ate plants on the ground and leaves from trees. It swallowed food whole. It ate stones to help digest its food.

Where the Apatosaurus Lived

Apatosaurus lived about 150 million years ago. This dinosaur probably lived on the forested plains of North America. It moved slowly.

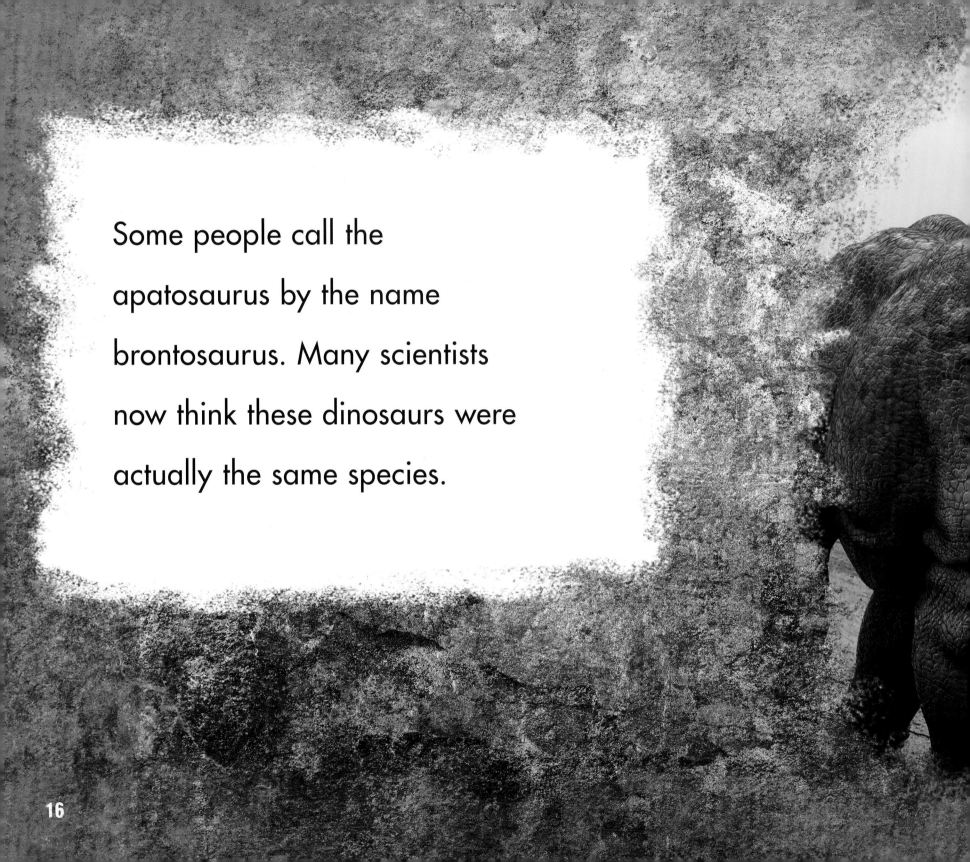

Some people call the apatosaurus by the name brontosaurus. Many scientists now think these dinosaurs were actually the same species.

A Fighting Chance

Apatosauruses probably got along well with other herbivores. But some dinosaur species hunted others. Scientists have found apatosaurus bones with teeth marks from other dinosaurs.

Apatosauruses sometimes fought each other. Scientists think the dinosaurs used their long necks in these battles. They may have also used their front claws to defend themselves.

Glossary

defend—to fight off an attack

digest—to break down food so it can be used by the body

herbivore—an animal that only eats plants

plain—a large, flat area of land with few trees

scientist—a person who studies the way the world works

species—a group of animals with similar features

Read More

Arlon, Penelope and Tory Gordon-Harris. *Dino Safari: A LEGO Adventure in the Real World.* Scholastic Readers. New York: Scholastic, 2016.

Lee, Sally. *Apatosaurus.* Little Explorers. North Mankato, Minn.: Capstone Press, 2015.

Pimentel, Annette Bay. *Do You Really Want to Meet Apatosaurus?* Do You Really Want to Meet a Dinosaur? Mankato, Minn.: Amicus Illustrated, 2018.

Internet Sites

Use FactHound to find Internet sites related to this book.

Visit www.facthound.com

Just type in 9781515795520 and go.

Super-cool stuff!

Check out projects, games and lots more at
www.capstonekids.com

Critical Thinking Questions

1. Why do you think the apatosaurus had such a long neck? What might it have helped the animal do?

2. Why do you think the apatosaurus lived on flat land?

3. Do you think other dinosaurs simply fought with the apatosaurus or hunted it for food? How might fossils help answer this question?

Index